About the Author

My name is Lynda Haffey, I live with my husband, John, my daughters, Olivia-Rose and Kate, a jug dog, Bonnie, goats, ducks and many chickens just outside Portadown, Co. Armagh. I am a freelance A-level geography teacher, hockey coach, keen runner, an avid yoga enthusiast and general lover of life. I truly hope you enjoy reading this book as much as I have loved writing it.
This is for the little bit of sloth inside all of us…

The Mindful Sloth

Lynda Haffey

The Mindful Sloth

Nightingale Books

Dedication

This book is dedicated to Partridge and Dilly Duck (The Originals)
Be Kind. Smile. Be Happy.

Acknowledgements

The writing of this book would not have been possible without the patience, encouragement and endless support of my family John, OR and MK.
Thank you x

ARCTIC OCEAN
NORTH AMERICA
EUROPE
ASIA
ATLANTIC OCEAN
PACIFIC OCEAN
AFRICA
PACIFIC OCEAN
SOUTH AMERICA
INDIAN OCEAN
AUSTRALIA
X - BORNEO

BRUNEI
MALAYSIA
BORNEO
INDONESIA

Deep in the jungle of Borneo,
Not so long but a while ago,
Lived a two toed sloth
Whose name was Bob,
And he snored and snuggled and snozzled and slobbed.

Bob the sloth could sleep all day
And often he did to others' dismay.
Dreaming and dozing up in the tree,
Toes gripping tightly for all to see.

For most of the day, with little exception,
Bob and his tree kept the tightest connection.
Nestled all cosy in his comfy spot,
Sumptuously serene, content with his lot.

The tree's upper canopy stretching so high,
Looked like a staircase right up to the sky,
And the clouds floating by like a giant marshmallow,
Squeezed out their raindrops like air from a bellow.

The jungle was bursting with all sorts of creatures,
An artist's bright canvas; a portrait of nature.
Tapirs, anacondas, panthers and monkeys,
Piranha, anteaters and birds of all species.

But none was so idle as the sloth brown and yellow,
This bundle of fur, this odd little fellow,
And so Bob the sloth, lazy, languid and listless,
Hung from the tree with the best of the vistas.

The toucan bird resplendent in colour,
Would go hunting aloft, leaving chicks with each other.
Yet the sloth in his lofty position up high,
Could easily keep watch with a careful eye.

The chicks, all secure in the nest near Bob's spot,
A ready made nursery, the best of the lot.
Safe from all predators cuddled in tight,
Bob took great care, both by day and by night.

But dangers were lurking in the forest so dark,
A fabulous feast tucked up snug in the bark.
A moment of carelessness, the chicks would be eaten,
A prize for the jaguar and Bob the sloth beaten.

So Bob the sloth would lie and stare,
And guard and groan and growl and glare.
Circling eagles would swoop too low,
Bob was guarding the chicks with his pointed toe.

Till Mum reappeared, her bill stuffed with lunch.
"Time now to eat, you hungry bunch.
Thanks for the day care," the toucan would cry.
"All part of the service," Bob the sloth would reply.

And as he perched in the tree, he sang to himself,
The forest's own radio, placed on a shelf.

"I'm a sloth as content as can be,
I love my life and I love my tree.
Don't call me lazy erroneously,
I'm happy in myself, I'm happy being me."

The old anaconda slithered up to the tree,
His jaw overstretched from a gluttonous tea.
Using the sloth as a luxurious mat,
He positioned himself, all bloated and fat.

"I've eaten too much," he said with a moan,
And he writhed and he whimpered aloud with a groan.
Using his toes, Bob massaged his belly,
And it slowly got soft like a bowlful of jelly.

His tummy relaxed and he felt much less sore,
The best ever day spa a snake could wish for.
And as he rubbed, Bob took time to advise,
Sounding so clever, so learned and wise.

"Don't just keep gobbling, hoovering up food,
It harms your digestion and does you no good.
And while we are chatting, may I just say,
It's important that you get your 5-a-day."

Bob broke into song as the happy snake listened
The scales on the skin of the snake brightly glistened.

"I'm a sloth as content as can be,
I love my life and I love my tree.
Don't call me lazy erroneously,
I'm happy in myself, I'm happy being me."

The piranha fish in the nearby river,
Was snappy and quick and an expert swimmer.
He was part of a group that was constantly fighting,
Picking and poking and annoyingly biting.

His teeth were sharp and spikey and jagged,
But all these rows had left him quite haggard.
He heard nothing else but the chattering of teeth,
Like a choir from the river, a song from beneath,
When suddenly something caught his attention,
And seemed to calm his inbuilt tension.

"Count your breaths... in... and out,"
Bob cajoled with an encouraging shout.
"All this conflict is bad for your health,
A happy community, now that is true wealth!

Inhale 1,2,3,4
Exhale 1,2,3,4,5,6

Inhale together... one... two... three,”
The sloth slowly counted. “Breathe like me,
And as you exhale, count for longer and longer
And the relaxation will feel even stronger.”

“This is called mindful meditation,
And needs to be practiced without hesitation.”
And just as he did this, piranha’s mood brightened
His spirits soared and his anxiety lightened.
And so piranha sidled up to the bank.
“You’re so clever, Bob, it’s you I must thank.”

Bob simply smiled as he broke into song
The fish in the river all sang along.

“I’m a sloth as content as can be,
I love my life and I love my tree.
Don’t call me lazy erroneously,
I’m happy in myself, I’m happy being me.”

Poison dart frog was a champion jumper,
Known in the forest as a resident thumper.
But jumping had left his leg muscle sore,
Bouncing around the rainforest floor.

He limped up to Bob with a pitiful cry,
And told of his woe with a sniff and a sigh.
"Hunting flies endlessly with no time to play
Means losing the very best part of the day."

Bob said to the frog, with care and compassion,
"Being busy all day is so out of fashion!
You must take time to stretch knees and achilles
When you jump from the bank to the pool with the lilies."

Bob led poison dart frog to a small forest clearing,
And with some instruction and plenty of cheering,
He pointed out places for fun all around,
A purpose built gym; the perfect playground.

"Lianas are vines that hang from the tree,
A perfectly good skipping rope, that is free."
So frog started jumping just for fun,
Giggling and chortling in the heat of the sun.
"Thank you, Bob, for your great advice,
Stretching my legs also feels nice."

"Keep up with the playtime," Bob said to the frog,
Singing out proudly splayed out on a log.

"I'm a sloth as content as can be,
I love my life and I love my tree.
Don't call me lazy erroneously,
I'm happy in myself, I'm happy being me."

Howler monkey was a real cheeky chap,
Who never ever would stop for a nap,
Constantly swinging through trees all the time,
Catching a ride by gripping each vine.

While Bob would watch with careful intent,
And position himself on the trees as he leant.
The perfect design of his fur on his back,
Would hang upside down and have the great knack,
Of helping the thirsty monkey take sips,
As the water ran down each of his drip tips.

And when thirsty and tired, the monkey below,
Would stretch out his tongue like the beak of a crow.
Bob said to the monkey, "If you're thirsty drink more,
eight glasses a day is the best to aim for."
"Thank you, Bob," said the monkey, "I was so dehydrated.
You're patient and kind and not irritated."

"Being cross gets you nowhere – isn't that what they say?"
Bob sang to the monkey as he started to sway.

"I'm a sloth as content as can be,
I love my life and I love my tree.
Don't call me lazy erroneously,
I'm happy in myself, I'm happy being me."

The hungry anteater with his pipe like nose,
Munched on termites all day, as they scurried too close.
He buried his snout into anthills with glee,
And snoffled and snorted while having his tea.

But constantly sniffing the forest floor,
Meant his poor old snoffle was bruised and sore.
He walked with a shuffle and ambled along,
With his gums all toothless and his nose so long.

Over exertion had left him tired,
And without his nose, he would soon be retired.
Anxious and weary, he visited Bob,
And with a blocked nose and a pitiful sob,
He told of his anguish and loss of smell,
The saddest of stories one never should tell.

"Sniffing all day is sore on my snout,
It's itchy and raw and all broken out.
My claws are broken from digging out hills,
Bob, can you help me... maybe some pills?"

Bob reached in his fur and pulled out a pot.
"This is for you, use the whole lot.
Plenty of rest and sloth balm for your nose,
Smear it all over and go for a doze.
And while you are here I will trim your claws."
And Bob slowly lifted the paws to his jaws.

As anteater smiled a toothless grin,
Bob pointed to the river, "Go on, get in!
It's not enough just to cream your nose,
It gets so much use as a vacuum hose!"

So anteater slid to the water so cool,
And slithered about in his own paddling pool.
Using his snout as a snorkel to breathe,
He frolicked about in the currents beneath.
"You need to make time to relax and chill out,
That's the only sure cure for a really sore snout."

Bob sang out his old familiar tune,
In his very own spotlight, lit up by the moon.

"I'm a sloth as content as can be,
I love my life and I love my tree.
Don't call me lazy erroneously,
I'm happy in myself, I'm happy being me."

Deep in the jungle of Borneo,
Hung Bob the sloth, idle and slow,
And the animals round him rushing so madly,
All stopped to listen, ever so gladly,
As he gathered them in, Bob spoke very gently,
And each of the animals listened intently.

"The very best parts of the day pass us by,
When we don't take time out to rest and shut eye.
Stop rushing around, seeing energies wasted,
Life is like food... if you gulp you can't taste it."

NEVER JUDGE
A BOOK
BY IT'S
COVER

For in any community we all play our part,
And give to the world the best of our hearts.
Bob the sloth could teach us all to pause,
And take care of others and be part of a cause.

As he gathered the animals all around,
They stared back at him, not making a sound.
"Sloths are creatures unlike any other,
But we must NEVER EVER judge a book by its cover!"

As he said this Bob slothfully stretched and yawned,
And to all the animals it suddenly dawned,
That each of them fully played a big part,
In this beautiful place, this pure work of art.

Lightning Source UK Ltd.
Milton Keynes UK
UKRC011347250821
389446UK00001B/4